EASTER
Vol. 49, No. 2

Publisher, Patricia A. Pingry
Associate Editor, D. Fran Morley
Art Director, Patrick McRae
Contributing Editors, Lansing Christman, Deana Deck, Russ Flint, Pamela Kennedy, Nancy J. Skarmeas, John Slobodnik
Editorial Assistant, Tim Hamling
ISBN 0-8249-1097-4

IDEALS—Vol. 49, No. 2 March MCMXCII IDEALS (ISSN 0019-137X) is published eight times a year: February, March, May, June, August, September, November, December by IDEALS PUBLISHING CORPORATION, P.O. Box 148000, Nashville, Tenn. 37214. Second-class postage paid at Nashville, Tennessee, and additional mailing offices. Copyright © MCMXCII by IDEALS PUBLISHING CORPORATION. POSTMASTER: Send address changes to Ideals, Post Office Box 148000, Nashville, Tenn. 37214-8000. All rights reserved. Title IDEALS registered U.S. Patent Office.

SINGLE ISSUE—$4.95
ONE-YEAR SUBSCRIPTION—eight consecutive issues as published—$19.95
TWO-YEAR SUBSCRIPTION—sixteen consecutive issues as published—$35.95
Outside U.S.A., add $6.00 per subscription year for postage and handling.

The cover and entire contents of IDEALS are fully protected by copyright and must not be reproduced in any manner whatsoever. Printed and bound in U.S.A.

TODAY from the book SONGS OF FAITH by Grace Noll Crowell. Copyright © 1939 by Harper and Brothers. Reprinted by permission of HarperCollinsPublishers. SPRING FEVER from the book THE PASSING THRONG by Edgar A. Guest: Used by permission of the author's estate. THE MOTHER OF OUR LORD from the book BESIDE STILL WATERS, by Edna Jaques: Published in Canada by Thomas Allen & Sons Limited. Used by permission. Our sincere thanks to the following whom we were unable to contact: Cora Louise Armor for LADY TULIP, Alberta Dodson for THE CHOIR, Eleanor Fiock for EASTER MESSAGE, Reginald Holmes for WHEN EASTER LILIES BLOOM.

Four-color separations by Rayson Films, Inc., Waukesha, Wisconsin
Printing by The Banta Company, Menasha, Wisconsin
Printed on Cougar by Weyerhauser

The paper used in this publication meets the minimum requirements of American National Standard for Information Sciences—Permanence of Paper for Printed Library Materials, ANSI Z39.48-1984.

Unsolicited manuscripts will not be returned without a self-addressed stamped envelope.

Inside front cover
Richard Hook

Inside back cover
John Walter

14	READERS' REFLECTIONS
18	TRAVELER'S DIARY
22	LEGENDARY AMERICANS
24	CRAFTWORKS
50	THROUGH MY WINDOW
52	READ TO ME
56	COLLECTOR'S CORNER
58	50 YEARS AGO
62	BITS AND PIECES
64	GARDEN-FRESH ASPARAGUS
66	COUNTRY CHRONICLE
70	SLICE OF LIFE
74	FROM MY GARDEN JOURNAL
80	READERS' FORUM

Written in March

William Wordsworth

The cock is crowing,
The stream is flowing,
The small birds twitter,
The lake doth glitter,
The green field sleeps in the sun;
The oldest and youngest
Are at work with the strongest;
The cattle are grazing,
Their heads never raising;
There are forty feeding like one!

Like an army defeated
The snow hath retreated,
And now doth fare ill
On the top of the bare hill;
The ploughboy is whooping—anon—anon—
There's joy in the mountains;
There's life in the fountains;
Small clouds are sailing,
Blue skies are prevailing;
The rain is over and gone!

Photo Opposite
DAFFODILS
G. Hampfler/H. Armstrong Roberts, Inc.

Heralds of Spring

Georgia B. Adams

The crocuses on tiptoes stood
Beside the garden wall—
The very first of springtime flowers
And then I heard their call:

"Awake, awake," they cried. "It's time
To toss the gloom away—
Bright tulips, golden daffodils
Arise, heed what we say!"

Sweet heralds closely nestled to
The breast of Mother Earth;
What lovely cups God has ordained
To usher in new birth.

Photo Opposite
GARDEN CROCUSES
G. Hampfler/H. Armstrong Roberts, Inc.

Cycles of Spring

May Smith White

Nature's unmatched cycles lie in wait—
As buds sleep quietly through protected care,
Not fearing spring's last frost, which might come late,
Each bud lies shielded, yet quite unaware.

BACKYARD AZALEA AND
DOGWOOD GARDEN
Louisville, Kentucky
Adam Jones Photography

As in time past, true nature's flow is sure,
Always unfolding in her rhythmic way—
The early violet, shy and demure,
Is proof against those things that will decay.

We welcome spring that follows winter's hush—
Though silences brought calm that we might know
These ever-changing scenes from nature's brush
Are needed, like the brilliant afterglow.
With spring's true-patterned cycle we will see
White crosses forming on the dogwood tree.

When Easter Lilies Bloom

Reginald Holmes

I marvel at God's handiwork
When Easter lilies bloom,
How such loveliness is raised
From winter's silent tomb.

I view with awe the artistry
Of every stalk and leaf,
Crowned with snow-white glory
That challenges belief;

And yet my faith is strengthened
For well I know that man
Will never reach the magnitude
Of God's creative plan;

And the old, inspiring story
Of empty cross and tomb
Has a new and deeper meaning
When Easter lilies bloom.

Photo Opposite
EASTER LILIES AND PINK HYDRANGEA
Bellingrath Gardens, Mobile, Alabama
Johnson's Photography

EASTER CHICKS
Diane Dietrich Leis Photography

April's a Child

Beverly J. Anderson

April's a child who likes to play,
Catching bright sunbeams on her way;
Skipping across the vales and hills
Waking the sleeping daffodils.

COTTONTAIL BUNNIES
Gay Bumgarner, Photographer

April's a child who likes to tease—
Sprinkling her showers, then to please
Sending blue skies and golden sun,
Opening blossoms one by one.

April's a child in emerald gown,
Wearing a rainbow-ribboned crown;
Blessing us with her gentle charms,
Bringing us lilacs in her arms.

April's a child of song and mirth
Spreading her joy o'er all the earth;
Thrilling our hearts to dance and sing,
Giving to us the gift of spring.

Lady Tulip

Cora Louise Armor

Lady Tulip, Lady Tulip,
As you raise your lovely head,
Lifting it in regal splendor
From your well-kept garden bed;
Do you know, oh, lovely lady,
In your cups, wine-red and gold,
Is a draught of inspiration—
Yet its quaffing you withhold.

Lady Tulip, Lady Tulip,
In whom Beauty sits enthroned,
Artists try in vain to paint you;
Their lament have they intoned.
In serene and queenly beauty,
In your cups, wine-red and gold,
You are holding poet's nectar—
Yet its quaffing you withhold.

Readers'

Lily of the Valley

Sweet Lily of the Valley
So special, Lord, to me.
Obscured three days in darkness
Arose in victory.

The tomb just could not hold You,
New life and love had won!
Your glorious Resurrection
Gave hope to everyone.

And now I hold a lily,
So fragrant, pure, and sweet,
Reminding me of You, Lord—
Your love eternally.

Anne B. Dodge
Brookhaven, Mississippi

Resurrection

Walking in the garden
On a crisp, clear day,
I marvelled at the beauty
All along the way.

In the chilly breeze
The little flowers shivered;
Hyacinths stood straight and tall,
While jonquils bowed and quivered.

The miracle of springtime—
My faith renewed again.
There is a resurrection
From death to life again.

Ellen Batson Watson
Greenville, South Carolina

Assurance

After the rain, the rainbow;
Beyond the clouds, the sun;
A reflection of love ever dawning
On a life that is just begun.

In darkness we must tarry,
Through turmoil we must trod;
A comfort ever present
Keeping us close to God.

After the rain, the rainbow;
Beyond the clouds, the sun;
A reflection of love ever dawning
On a life that is just begun.

Linda Royahn Copper
Baltimore, Maryland

Reflections

'Tis Spring

The day is as young as a newborn child;
The morning air is clear and mild.

Flowers are brilliantly blooming nearby
And welcome a visit from a butterfly.

A slight, caring breeze blows through the trees
Giving soft motion to all the new leaves.

Clouds appear in front of my eyes
And form puffy pillows in bright blue skies.

A bird sings its song, as if to say,
"Thank you, Lord, for this beautiful day."

> Shirley Ester
> Dothan, Alabama

April

April's a spirit
    with warm, gentle showers
Who coaxes from slumber
    the lovely Spring flowers.

And then with a wave
    of her magical wand,
All life sings an anthem
    on meadow and pond.

While high in the clouds
    a banner unfurled,
Proclaims resurrection,
    the soul of the world.

> Lois Graf
> Lancaster, Ohio

Easter Glory

Elisabeth Weaver Winstead

Easter dawns early, tranquil and bright,
Aglow in a heavenly, radiant light.

Easter bells chiming in triumph are ringing,
In echoing anthems of angels' soft singing.

The early spring crocus and gold daffodil
Are spreading fresh blossoms
  on every green hill.

Homing birds nesting in tall, leafy trees
In splendor performing
  their rare symphonies.

The wonder of Easter unfolds in its story,
Proclaiming life's promise of eternal glory.

Hearts overflowing in reverence give voice,
"The Lord is risen! In praise, we rejoice!"

TRAVELER'S Diary

Nancy J. Skarmeas

H. Armstrong Roberts, Inc.

The Mission at San Juan Capistrano

The church at San Juan Capistrano was one of the most magnificent of all the Spanish missions built in the American West. Constructed of sandstone carried to the site by Indian parishioners in horse-drawn carts, the church stretched one hundred and eighty feet and was topped by seven domes. The bell tower rose over one hundred feet into the clear southern California sky and housed four bells whose music was heard throughout the surrounding countryside. The church was completed in 1806, and for the next six years the Spanish padres gathered the local Indians within its walls for instruction and worship.

The church was a shining example of man's greatest works in service of his highest purposes, but such consecrated beginnings did not protect San Juan Capistrano from the destructive forces

H. Armstrong Roberts, Inc.

San Juan Capistrano was one of twenty-one Franciscan missions founded in California between 1769 and 1825. The missions served a dual purpose for the Spanish in spreading Christianity to the Native Americans of the area as well as providing a political stronghold in the still unclaimed western territory. Each mission was to continue for ten years, during which time the padres would instruct the natives in Christianity and agricultural self-sufficiency. When the ten years had passed, the mission was to be turned over to the local people as a self-governing Spanish colony.

Spanish political control over the region did not last, but the missions developed into one of the single most influential forces in the development of the state. California grew up around the missions. Its architecture, its place names, and even the locations of its major cities are a reflection of the Spanish padres and their work. Many Californians also believe that the spirit of welcome which their state has always extended to travelers and settlers alike is the legacy of the padres who opened their missions to weary and hungry travelers in the days when California was mostly wild and only sparsely populated.

These days, San Juan Capistrano is known as much for its swallows as for its mission. The birds' return each year brings worldwide attention to the area and inspires observers with thoughts of the mysterious cycles of nature that govern our lives. But visitors looking for evidence of life's continuity can find similar inspiration at the local mission. The once-grand church is now in ruins, but the beautiful gardens that surround it provide a peaceful setting for reflection or prayer. And the bells that once pealed across miles of countryside now intone softly as the breeze moves the ropes attached to their clappers; but their sound is no less appealing for its softness. Out of the long-ago destruction of San Juan Capistrano has arisen a simple, peaceful place for reflection, a place that in its simple beauty reminds visitors not only of the fragility of even the most well-intentioned of man's works, but also of life's stubborn insistence on rebirth and renewal in the face of death and destruction.

of nature. On a December day in 1812, a tremendous earthquake shook the region, bringing the church's carefully constructed walls crashing down on the very people who had labored to raise them. When the earth was quiet, the church was in ruins and forty lives had been lost. The work of the mission was to continue, but the beautiful sandstone church was never rebuilt.

Today, although the ruins of the church remain as a reminder of the violent destruction of almost two hundred years ago, San Juan Capistrano is a beautiful and peaceful place. The ruins of the once-magnificent church are now surrounded by lush green gardens, and the bells that once rang from the heights of the tower now hang in the walls of a small adobe church. This modest church was the original place of worship at the mission and is today the oldest surviving building in California. The mission, located between Los Angeles and San Diego, is a favorite stop for travelers, providing both a respite from the crowds in the big cities and a glance into the state's unique past.

Easter

Kay Hoffman

Although it happened long ago,
That first glad Easter day;
Within the true believer's heart,
It's just as real today.

The Roman guards who kept the watch,
The early morning gloom,
The angel's words, "He is not here"
Resounding from the tomb.

And oh, the joy in Mary's heart
While in the garden fair
To see her blessed Lord appear
Upon the pathway there.

Although it happened long ago,
It still is true today;
Oh, let our hearts rejoice and sing,
The stone is rolled away.

Nancy J. Skarmeas

Roger Williams

In January of 1636, a group of Puritans led by Captain John Underhill sailed out of Boston Harbor and headed north toward Salem and the home of Roger Williams. Williams, a minister who the previous October had stood trial on the charge of "maintaining dangerous opinions," had been warned to cease his preaching or face banishment from the colony and deportation to England. For the passionate Williams, the sentence had proven unbearable, and when word reached Boston that he was again promoting the cause of religious freedom and tolerance among the members of his former congregation, his days as a citizen of Massachusetts were numbered.

Yet the Puritan leaders were never to have the satisfaction of seeing Williams board a ship bound for England; before Underhill and his men reached Salem, Williams had received word of their intentions and fled on his own. Leaving his wife, children, and home behind, he headed south, into the foreboding New England winter wilderness and out of the boundaries of the suddenly dangerous Massachusetts. For fourteen weeks Williams struggled against cold and starvation; but when spring broke, he was alive and well, and he planted the first crops in a new settlement on land secured from the Narragansett Indians. He called his new home Providence.

Judging from the fervor with which the Puritans pursued Williams, one might imagine that he was a dangerous heretic. On the contrary, Roger Williams himself had been a dedicated and popular Puritan minister at the time of his arrival in Massachusetts four years earlier. He had arrived in the colony with glowing recommendations and great expectations.

It was not long, however, before the Puritan officials in Massachusetts began wondering about the man they had welcomed so readily, and Roger Williams began to realize that the church in New England was not as far removed from the church he left in England.

Both Williams and the original settlers of Massachusetts had come to New England for the same reason. Both believed that power and politics had corrupted the church in England, and both believed that it was their mission to found a pure church in the New World. For the Puritans, the new church was to be a branch of the old, a pure seed planted beyond the reach of the old corruption, that would eventually purify the whole church body. But Williams was a separatist. He believed that the church in England was beyond saving and that the church in New England must sever all ties with the old or fall victim to the very same corruption.

The question of separation was a main point of contention, but it was not the only one, nor did it alone guarantee Williams' banishment from the colony. It was his views on religious freedom and tolerance that convinced the Puritans that Roger Williams was a threat. For Williams, religious truth was something pure and exalted—something beyond the realm of secular governments. The Puritans, in their efforts to create the model religious community—their "city upon a hill"—sought to control every aspect of the lives of each and every citizen. Roger Williams preached tolerance, based on the assumptions that human laws and punishments had no bearing on God's truth and that an individual need only be concerned with his own salvation and not with passing judgment on others. Williams spoke out against Puritan oppression and called for the acceptance of dissenting voices—not as an admission of weakness but as a proof of strength.

Williams' message of tolerance proved too much for the Puritans; and before he had the chance to spread his beliefs, he was gone. Others, facing similar oppression, soon followed Williams to Providence, which became a haven for those seeking freedom of religious belief. After a few years in Providence, Williams became a Baptist and founded the first Baptist church in America; but his devotion to this denomination lasted only a few months. Williams could not be satisfied with an organized religion that necessarily included manmade rules and restrictions. From that point on, Roger Williams referred to himself as a "seeker," a Christian believer not yet satisfied with any organized church.

It was not too long after Williams' departure that things began to fall apart in his former colony. Their restrictive ways created many an outsider, so many that soon the outsiders outnumbered the insiders and the pure Puritan state was just another colony governed not by religious but by secular law.

Many today like to see Roger Williams as a forerunner of Thomas Jefferson. Such a comparison, while certainly flattering to Williams, also does him an injustice. Thomas Jefferson's concern was, rightly, the formation of a secular nation; Williams' concern was religious truth. They both sought separation of church and state: Jefferson for the sake of the state and Williams for the sake of religion. Williams, in fact, thought little of the form and foundation of secular governments as long as they did not lay claim to the realm of religious truth. Williams did not covet fame or power, simply the freedom to seek God in his own way. By doing so with an unwavering faith and the courage to defend it, he began a tradition of tolerance still cherished in America.

CRAFTWORKS

Gingerbread Church at Eastertime

Martha Goodlow

Because of limited space, we have not listed ingredients or supplies needed to complete this church. Before beginning, please read directions and make a list of everything you will need. Trace pattern pieces as indicated on this page. Cut additional pattern pieces as follows:

- 2 roof sides: 5½ by 10 inches
- 2 walls: 9 by 4 inches (cut 3 window openings in each wall, following photo)
- 1 belfry base: 3 inches square
- 2 belfry sides: 2 by 2½ inches
- 2 belfry arches: 2 by 2½ inches with arches cut as in assembly diagram
- 2 watchtower sides: 2½ inches square
- 1 spire base: 2½ inches square
- 1 step: 1 by 3½ inches

Make two batches of Gingerbread using the following recipe. In a large bowl, combine 5 cups flour and 1 tablespoon baking soda; set aside. Cream 1 cup margarine (not butter) with 1 cup dark brown sugar. Stir in 1 tablespoon each cinnamon and ginger, 2 tablespoons salt, 1 teaspoon allspice, 1 cup unsulphured molasses, and 2 lightly beaten eggs. Add flour, a little at a time, stirring after each addition. Stir to a smooth dough and chill several hours.

For the windows, crush several different colors of hard candy and set aside. Preheat oven to 350°. Roll out dough on a lightly floured surface to ¼ inch thick. Lay out the pattern pieces, and cut around each with a sharp knife. Bake on a greased baking sheet 10 to 12 minutes, or until firm to the touch. Cool on a wire rack. **For walls with windows:** Bake side and back walls on a foil-lined baking sheet. After 8 minutes, fill empty windows with the crushed candy. Return to oven and bake an additional 4 to 5 minutes, or until candy is melted. Cool on wire rack; peel foil from back.

Make icing. Combine 1 pound confectioners' sugar, 1 tablespoon softened butter, and ½ teaspoon vanilla extract. Gradually stir in ⅓ cup milk. Frost steeple pieces with icing and sprinkle with nonpareils. Allow to dry.

ASSEMBLING THE CHURCH

Use green styrofoam or painted board for a base; for location, mark a 6- by 9-inch rectangle. Pipe icing on bottom and inside edges of walls. Set on base according to marks, and hold in place until icing hardens. Reinforce seams with icing.

Pipe icing on sloping edges of front and back walls and inside of roof pieces. Press roof in place and let dry completely.

Assemble steeple by following diagram. Pipe icing on inside edges of watchtower's front and back walls. Press side walls to front wall, and back wall to side walls. Pipe icing along top edges; attach belfry floor. Pipe icing on 3 edges of belfry's front, sides, and back walls. Attach to belfry's floor and hold until firm. Before attaching spire's base, carefully make a small hole in the center of the base. Cut a 4-inch length of ribbon and fasten with icing to top of a foil-wrapped HERSHEY'S KISS®. Push ribbon through hole in base and knot so "bell" is positioned correctly in belfry. Pipe icing around top edges of belfry walls; attach steeple base. Set aside.

On edges of spire, pipe icing; assemble and hold until set. Pipe icing on bottom edges of steeple and set on base. Pipe icing in any spaces and let steeple tower dry completely.

Pipe icing along bottom inside edges of assembled tower; place on peak of roof.

To shingle the roof, pipe a dot of icing in middle of a candy wafer and press in place along bottom edge of roof. Overlap succeeding rows, working toward peak, until roof is covered.

For front step, pipe icing around bottom edge and position as shown. Trim church with piped icing as in photo.

If desired, landscape as shown using green tinted icing and coconut. Trees are paper cones frosted with a leaf-shaped tip. Spearmint leaf candy serves as small bushes. Add vines and flowers of tinted icing if desired.

Photo Opposite
GINGERBREAD EASTER CHURCH
Ron Little/Rush Photography

Easter Morn

Georgia B. Adams

See them lined up in a row
Here in church on Easter morn
Sitting in the family pew
From oldest boy to one just born,

Mom and Dad at either end;
See them dressed so trim and neat
Girls beribboned, boys with ties
As so quietly they meet.

Sunday mornings year around
See them fill the family pew
Families all together praying
Mother, Dad and children too.

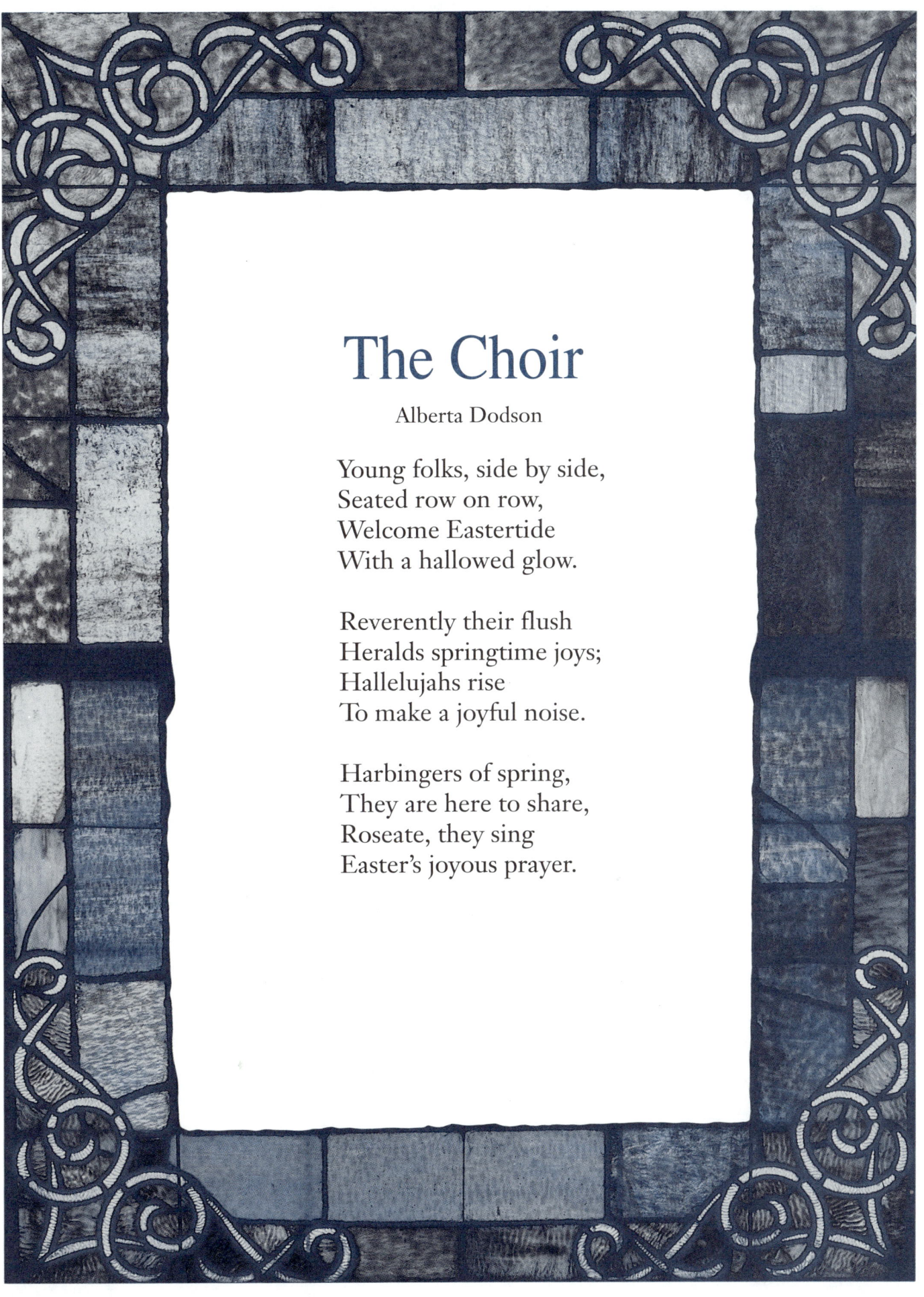

The Choir

Alberta Dodson

Young folks, side by side,
Seated row on row,
Welcome Eastertide
With a hallowed glow.

Reverently their flush
Heralds springtime joys;
Hallelujahs rise
To make a joyful noise.

Harbingers of spring,
They are here to share,
Roseate, they sing
Easter's joyous prayer.

A Child's Thought of God

Elizabeth Barrett Browning

They say that God lives very high!
  But if you look above the pines
You cannot see our God. And why?

And if you dig down in the mines
  You never see Him in the gold,
Though from Him all that's glory shines.

God is so good, He wears a fold
  Of heaven and earth across His face—
Like secrets kept, for love untold.

But still I feel that His embrace
Slides down by thrills, through all things made,
Through sight and sound of every place:

As if my tender mother laid
  On my shut lids her kisses' pressure,
Half-waking me at night and said,
  "Who kissed you through the dark,
  dear guesser?"

Easter Message

Eleanor Fiock

Easter brings a message
In flowers and in song,
A message full of gladness
To cheer the waiting throng.

Easter brings a message
At dawn on sunrise hill;
The stone has rolled away all doubt
For Christ is living still.

Easter brings a message,
It's told from sea to sea—
The angels chant the tidings:
"Christ lives in you and me."

Photo Opposite
MIDWAY CHURCH
Midway, Georgia
Ken Dequaine Photography

The Mother of Our Lord

Edna Jaques

I wonder if the mother of our Lord,
   Fussed over little rugs and warmed her bread,
Hung clean washed clothes beneath the sunny sky,
   Made pretty quilts to lie upon His bed.

I wonder if she laid the supper fire
   And put the kettle on to warm for tea,
Used her good dishes for His birthday feast,
   Cradled His tired head against her knee.

I wonder if she ever talked to Him
   About the shepherds and the things they said,
And told Him how they came that wondering night
   To gather 'round His little humble bed.

Or told Him in her wise and gentle way,
   The message that the angels brought to her,
The little stable at the edge of town,
   The lovely gift of frankincense and myrrh,

Ah yes, I know—she pondered all these things
   Against her heart—and talked as mothers will,
(Sensing no sword above her quiet hearth
   No shadow of a cross against a hill.)

The Triumphant Entry

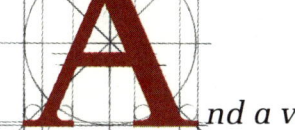

*And a very
great multitude spread their garments
in the way; others cut down branches
from the trees, and strawed
them in the way.
And the multitudes that went before,
and that followed, cried, saying,
Hosanna to the son of David:
Blessed is he that cometh
in the name of the Lord;
Hosanna in the highest.*

*And when he was come into Jerusalem,
all the city was moved, saying,
Who is this?
And the multitude said,
This is Jesus
the prophet of Nazareth
of Galilee.*

MATTHEW 21: 8-11

The Last Supper

And the first
day of unleavened bread, his disciples said unto
him, Where wilt thou that we go and prepare
that thou mayest eat the passover?
And he sendeth forth two of his disciples,
and saith unto them, Go ye into the city,
and there shall meet you a man
bearing a pitcher of water: follow him.
And he will shew you a large upper room
furnished and prepared:
there make ready for us.

And as they did eat, Jesus took bread, and blessed,
and brake it, and gave to them, and said, Take,
eat: this is my body. And he took
the cup, and when he had given thanks,
he gave it to them: and they all drank of it.
And he said unto them,
This is my blood of the new testament,
which is shed for many.
And when they had sung an hymn,
they went out into the mount of Olives.

MARK 14: 12, 13, 15, 22-24, 26

Photo Opposite
THE LAST SUPPER
Gustav Wegener
1817-1877

The Garden

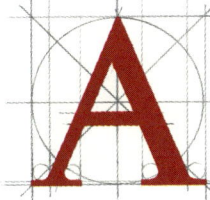nd they came
to a place which was named Gethsemane:
and he saith to his disciples,
Sit ye here, while I shall pray. . . .
My soul is exceeding sorrowful unto death:
tarry ye here, and watch.

And he went forward a little, and fell on the
ground, and prayed that, if it were possible,
the hour might pass from him.
And he said, Abba, Father,
all things are possible unto thee;
take away this cup from me: nevertheless
not what I will, but what thou wilt.

. . . the hour is come;
behold, the Son of man
is betrayed into the hands of sinners.
Rise up, let us go;
lo, he that betrayeth me is at hand.

Mark 14: 32, 34-36, 41, 42

Photo Opposite
THE AGONY IN THE GARDEN
Andrea Mantegna
1431-1506

The Trial

ow at that
feast the governor was wont to release unto the
people a prisoner, whom they would.
And they had then a notable prisoner,
called Barabbas. . . . Pilate said unto them,
Whom will ye that I release unto you?
Barabbas, or Jesus which is called Christ?
They said, Barabbas. Pilate saith unto them,
What shall I do then with
Jesus which is called Christ?
They all say unto him, Let him be crucified.
And the governor said, Why, what evil hath he
done? But they cried out the more, saying,
Let him be crucified.

When Pilate saw that he could prevail nothing,
but that rather a tumult was made,
he took water, and washed his hands
before the multitude, saying, I am innocent of the
blood of this just person:
see ye to it.

MATTHEW 27: 15-17, 21-24

Photo Opposite
CHRIST BEFORE PILATE
Jacopo Tintoretto
1518-1594

The Crucifixion

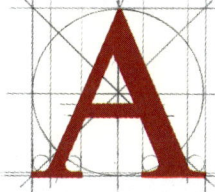nd they bring him unto the place Golgotha, which is, being interpreted, The place of a skull. And when they had crucified him, they parted his garments, casting lots upon them, what every man should take. And it was the third hour. . . . And with him they crucify two thieves; the one on his right hand, and the other on his left. And the scripture was fulfilled, which saith, And he was numbered with the transgressors. And at the ninth hour Jesus cried with a loud voice, saying. . . . My God, my God, why hast thou forsaken me? And Jesus cried with a loud voice, and gave up the ghost. And the veil of the temple was rent in twain. . . . And when the centurion, which stood over against him, saw that he so cried out, and gave up the ghost, he said, Truly this man was the Son of God.

MARK 15: 22, 24, 25, 27, 28, 34, 37-39

Photo Opposite
CHRIST ON THE CROSS
Ferdinand Delecroix
1798-1863

The Triumph

ow upon
the first day of the week, very early in the
morning, they came unto the sepulchre,
bringing the spices which they had prepared,
and certain others with them.
And they found the stone rolled away from the
sepulchre. And they entered in, and found not
the body of the Lord Jesus.

And it came to pass, as they were much perplexed
thereabout, behold, two men
stood by them in shining garments:
And . . . said unto them,
Why seek ye the living among the dead?
He is not here, but is risen: remember how he
spake unto you when he was yet in Galilee,
Saying, the Son of man must be delivered into the
hands of sinful men, and be crucified,
and the third day rise again.
And they remembered his words . . .
and told all these things unto . . . the rest.

LUKE 24: 1-8

Photo Opposite
THREE MARYS AT THE TOMB
Adolphe William Bouguereau
1825-1905

The Ascension

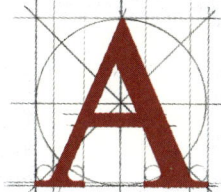nd he said
unto them, These are the words
which I spake unto you
while I was yet with you,
that all things must be fulfilled, which were
written in the law of Moses,
and in the prophets, and in the psalms,
concerning me. Then opened he their
understanding, that they might understand
the scriptures, And said unto them,
Thus it is written, and thus it behoved Christ
to suffer, and to rise from the dead
the third day:

And ye are witnesses of these things.
And he led them out as far as to Bethany,
and he lifted up his hands, and blessed them.
And it came to pass, while he blessed them,
he was parted from them, and carried up into
heaven. And they worshipped him,
and returned to Jerusalem with great joy:
And were continually in the temple,
praising and blessing God.
Amen.

Luke 24: 44-46, 48, 50-53

THROUGH MY WINDOW
— Pamela Kennedy

I am John, a fisherman, the son of a fisherman, the brother of a fisherman. Years ago I saw before me the life of my father and brother, stretching as wide and clear as the Sea of Galilee. There were nets to mend and boats to repair, fish to be sorted and sold. Life had a texture as comforting and reliable as the passing of seasons.

Then he came. He called, "Follow me" and we could hear no other voices; not the sea, not our friends, not even our father and mother. And so my brother James and I left the nets and followed him, unsure of our motivation, knowing only that we could not resist his call. We would become fishers of men, he said. We didn't know what he meant, but we followed just the same.

He called others too until there were twelve of us. Not all were fishermen. Some were learned, some were not—we were philosophers, businessmen, tradesmen, rebels. But we were all seekers and we followed him looking for answers, even before we had fully formed the questions.

For three years we walked and talked and lived with him as he taught us things unfamiliar to our Galilean minds. It was not always easy to understand him, but he was patient like a father working with an eager, but less-than-brilliant child. And we tried to learn and understand because we loved him more than our own lives.

Then he left us. It happened almost before we knew it, although we should have known. The signs were there all along. Always under the surface lurked the hatred, the anger, the scent of murder waiting for its hour. But love never wants to believe in evil and so we refused to see the signs. We talked of faithfulness and greatness in a kingdom yet to come and he spoke of suffering and crucifixion and we ignored him. But he knew. He always knew.

When they came, led by the traitor, Judas, to take him away, we scattered like frightened children. Long forgotten were our vows of loyalty. We left our promises in the dark of Gethsemane.

He went freely, although they thought they took him by force. And when he stood before the magistrates, I hid in shadows and heard his words. He spoke the truth, yet they didn't understand anymore than I had at first. And they hated him because he would not bow before their petty power.

Peter denounced him loudly just as the rooster crowed. But I, in my refusal to speak, denounced him too. Some thought my silence strength, but he and I knew it was not. It was fear as raw and bold as blood.

They marched him to Golgotha and we few followers clung together in our grief. I watched his mother's face and marveled at its serenity, even as tears streamed down her cheeks. I longed to speak but did not. I wanted to shout my love for him but could not. Somehow, he lifted his poor, anguished head and said, "Here is your mother." I took her home that day after the agony of his death, wondering at the trust he placed in me, overcome with gratitude.

There was nothing to do, we thought, but gather together and pray. But our prayers seemed as lifeless as his body, and the days continued, broken only by restless sleep.

Then on the morning of the third day, the women came running, gasping with news of angels and a resurrection. Their words tumbled out in excitement and we determined them hysterical. But something in their eyes gripped my heart. I caught Peter's glance and we ran to the garden tomb.

I arrived there first, but could not enter, paralyzed by awe and fear. I stood, transfixed, my hand upon unyielding stone, peering in. I saw the strips of linen on the bier, but did not comprehend their import. Then Peter pushed past me roughly. His shout of alarm pulled me forward from my fear, and slowly, tentatively, I entered that place of death.

The morning light streamed in and settled on the empty graveclothes. He was not there! The realization fell on me like the dawning sun. We did not speak; there were no words to clarify our emotions. We ran from the tomb laughing like children, seeing the world afresh like blind men healed!

In the emptiness of that stony grave I found fulfillment not only of my life, but of all the promises he had made. Slowly I began to see the sense of it; the stories, parables, prophecies and prayers weaving together in a tapestry of truth.

And then he came again! He showed himself to us and taught us deeper things we had not understood before. Our grief was gone. The answer to our prayers stood before us and we walked and talked with him once more. His bright and shining truth drove all doubts out of our minds. Now we could truly fish for men and serve our Master well. Denial, failure, abandonment were forgiven once and always.

He departed once more, rising in the morning sky and we watched him go in glory, but were not sad. We will see him again, each in his appointed time. But now we trace the paths before us, laid out by his hand with love and care. I walk now, hearing only two words: "Follow me."

Pamela Kennedy is a freelance writer of short stories, articles, essays, and children's books. Married to a naval officer and mother of three children, she has made her home on both U.S. coasts and in Hawaii and currently resides in Washington, D.C. She draws her material from her own experiences and memories, adding bits of imagination to create a story or mood.

Art by Russ Flint

All Things Bright and Beautiful

Cecil Frances Alexander

All things bright and beautiful,
  All creatures, great and small,
All things wise and wonderful,
  The Lord God made them all.

Each little flower that opens,
  Each little bird that sings,
He made their glowing colors,
  He made their tiny wings;

The rich man in his castle,
  The poor man at his gate,
God made them, high or lowly,
  And ordered their estate.

The purple-headed mountain,
  The river running by,
The sunset, and the morning
  That brightens up the sky;

The cold wind in the winter,
  The pleasant summer sun,
The ripe fruits in the garden—
  He made them every one.

The tall trees in the greenwood,
  The meadows where we play,
The rushes by the water
  We gather every day,—

He gave us eyes to see them,
  And lips that we might tell
How great is God Almighty,
  Who has made all things well!

Mama's Easter Bonnet

Beatrice Wheeler Baier

It was Easter Sunday morning,
And Mama had a bonnet,
A mountain of pink flowers
With bows and ribbons on it.

We girls all had pink dresses,
And we got up bright and early,
And Mama used the curling iron
To make our hair all curly.

While Mama helped us dress
And tied each satin sash,
Father put his white shirt on
And waxed his long mustache.

While Mama brushed our curls
And tied them up with bows,
Father rubbed his shiny shoes
And brushed his brand-new clothes.

When all the girls were ready,
Ribboned, brushed and dressed,
Father draped his watch-chain
Festoon-like on his vest.

But Mama hadn't time
To do justice to her bonnet,
So quickly pushing back her hair,
She popped her bonnet on it.

She stuck it with a hat pin,
And we were on our way,
On Easter Sunday morning,
A lovely April day.

Father was so proud,
Impeccably he'd dressed.
Mama looked at Father,
And she was quite impressed.

When the last hymn had been sung,
And we rose to leave our pew,
A lady talked with Mama . . .
It was then that Mama knew!

The lady said to Mama
That she liked her bonnet so,
But wasn't it just backward
Of the way it ought to go?

Oh, yes it was! Poor Mama!
She had worked on us so long
That she hadn't time to notice
That her bonnet was on wrong.

COLLECTOR'S CORNER

D. Fran Morley

Easter Seals

As many collectors know, an item does not need to have a particular monetary worth to be an interesting collectible. Often, an item's beauty, sentimental value, or original purpose is enough to make it valuable to the collector. And if an item possesses all three attributes, as do Easter Seals, it is especially rewarding to collect.

Easter Seals, the most recognizable symbol of the Easter Seal Society, first appeared in 1934; but the society has been around much longer. The Ohio Society for Crippled Children, the forerunner of today's organization, was founded in 1919 by businessman Edgar Allen after his young son was killed in a streetcar accident. The movement gradually spread throughout the United States, at first benefitting only crippled children but later adults as well. The organization's name changed several times over the years; but in 1967 it became The Easter Seal Society, in recognition of the valuable part Easter Seals play in the organization. Today, despite the success of an annual telethon and other fund raising events, the Easter Seal campaign continues to be the Society's largest source of contributed income.

The first seals were designed by J.H. Donahey, a well-known cartoonist at the *Cleveland Plain Dealer* in Cleveland, Ohio, in 1934. He wanted to create a miniature poster to attract attention to the Society's services and increase donations by giving the public something in exchange for its contributions. Easter was chosen as the theme for the seals because of the connection between new life and rehabilitation. In introducing Donahey's Easter Seal, Paul H. King, the president of the Society, stated, "Thoughts of Easter and the child with disabilities harmonize wonderfully. Easter means, of course, resurrection and new life, and certainly the rehabilitation of children means . . . new life and activity, complete or partial, physically, mentally and spiritually."

The new Easter Seals were an immediate success and have continued to be appreciated as the miniature posters that their creator imagined. Designed by staff members or an outside advertising agency, Easter Seals featured a variety of styles over the years, most including some variation of a child with an Easter lily. Some of the seals are cute, the childlike drawings from 1962, for example; others, such as the continuous lily design from 1968, are very elegant. Usually, there are only one or two stamp designs; but in 1991 there were six different lily seals.

Although their appearance is similar to postage stamps, Easter Seals and their like, such as wildlife stamps or stamps from Boys Town or the Disabled American Veterans, are not considered valuable collectibles by serious stamp collectors and will not be found at most stamp shows or stores. The best place to find Easter Seals is at estate sales or auctions. Examine old

letters carefully since, on occasion, old envelopes will have Easter Seals firmly attached. Most collectors prefer to collect whole sheets, although these are harder to find than the individual seals. But of course, a collection can be started with new seals, since new designs of Easter Seals are released every spring.

Framed and matted, an entire sheet of Easter Seals, particularly one like the continuous lily design, make a lovely wall decoration. Individual seals grouped by year, color, or style also look pretty framed. For more personal viewing, a collection can be kept in a small photo album or scrapbook.

However they are displayed, Easter Seals, with their beauty, sentimental value, and purpose, are as meaningful today as when they were first introduced. Today, as in 1934, they represent the public's willingness to support new life through rehabilitation.

Stamps Courtesy Easter Seal Society of Tennessee, Inc.

50 Years Ago

Victory Bikes

Plans are afoot to make bicycle riding a required sport at Harvard University. This is not so funny as some of the more muscular members of its athletic menage seem to imagine. Take it from Harold Frankel, a Harvard man himself. In undergraduate days, a strong and nimble exponent of the catch-as-catch-can school of intercollegiate wrestling, Mr. Frankel now has a half-nelson on a bicycle business partnership in Harvard Square, handling some 15,000 rentals a year.

Bicycling, Mr. Frankel asserts, is sure to become required sport for millions of adult Americans.

This view is borne out by the lively effect automobile tire and gasoline restrictions have had on bicycle sales and rentals in recent weeks. It is significant that just when Secretary Ickes was about to toll official curfew on New England gas stations, bicycle dealers throughout that area were telling people the sad news about a sudden bicycle shortage.

Sales folk in department and retail mailorder stores, hardware and sporting goods places, pointed to racks depleted of all but a few underslung, overweight models freighted with gadgets and brightwork designed to catch the fifth-grade eye. And right when the run was on full tilt, the

very British dealer in Boston for a celebrated Manchester bike maker was seen trying to hold off an incipient mob with one left-over, little-girl's model.

Certainly the War Production Board's order of April 2, freezing all bicycle sales until a rationing system can be worked out, did not take the public by surprise.

The Victory bike, as the WPB calls the wartime model, made its debut in a special television broadcast late in March. Apparently there's a lot of engineering refinement secreted in its general design. The first thing you notice about the Victory model is its lightness. The official limitation order restricts the bike to 31 pounds.

The weight factor has a two-way advantage. Primarily, it is intended to save critical metals for the war industry. The WPB estimates that the standardized, gadgetless model will net a saving of 22 tons of nickel, 17 tons of tin, 590 tons of copper and alloys, 5 tons of cadmium, and steel enough to build 1,300 army tanks. The lightweight Victory will also save "wear and tear" on the rider. Any seasoned bicycle tourist will tell you, the lighter the bike the easier the trip.

The WPB sanctioned the Victory with an eye to the greater general need for transportation no less than recreation. No manufacturer can make a bike that measures less than 20 inches from the crank hub to the top of the saddle-post staff. This is definitely an adult dimension. It means the government has practically forbidden the making of children's bicycles for the duration.

Youngsters who can work the Victory's 20-inch reach may not think much of this olive-drab, pneumaticized gazelle, considering their pretty general liking for a bike that looks like a motor-cycle. But a good many thousand grown-ups in war factories, who won't be able to drive cars much longer, are all set to pedal their way to where the Victory bike implies that America is heading.

from *The Christian Science Monitor* April 25, 1942

We Thank Thee

Anonymous

For mother-love and father-care,
For brothers strong and sisters fair,
For love at home and here each day,
For guidance lest we go astray,
Father in heaven, we thank Thee.

For this new morning with its light,
For rest and shelter of the night,
For health and food, for love and friends,
For ev'rything His goodness sends,
Father in heaven, we thank Thee.

For flowers that bloom about our feet,
For tender grass, so fresh, so sweet,
For song of bird and hum of bee,
For all things fair we hear or see,
Father in heaven, we thank Thee.

For blue of stream and blue of sky,
For pleasant shade of branches high,
For fragrant air and cooling breeze,
For beauty of the blooming trees,
Father in heaven, we thank Thee.

Bits & Pieces

Come, ye saints, look here and wonder,
See the place where Jesus lay;
He has borne our sins away;
Joyful tiding,
Yes, the Lord has risen today.

                Thomas Kelly

I believe in the brook as it wanders
  From hillside in to glade;
I believe in the breeze as it whispers
  When evening's shadows fade.

I believe in the faith of the flowers;
  I believe in the rock and sod,
For in all of these appearth clear
  The handiwork of God.

                Anonymous

Hallelujah! Hallelujah!
On the third morning He arose,
Bright with victory o'er his foes.
  Sing we lauding,
  And applauding,
  Hallelujah!

    From the Latin of the 12th Century

Through years, as April comes, I know
That I shall watch each budding flower
And feel again the balm that comes
To those who wait this holy hour.

                May Smith White

"Christ the Lord is risen today,"
Sons of men and angels say.
Raise your joys and triumphs high;
Sing, ye heavens, and earth reply.

                Charles Wesley

The barrier stone has rolled away,
  And loud the angels sing;
The Christ comes forth this blessed day
  To reign, a deathless king.
For shall we not believe He lives
  Through such awakening?
Behold, how God each April gives
  The miracle of spring.

                Edwin L. Sabin

Chime, solemn bells of Easter!
  The shadows flee away,
And all the earth is smiling
  In the glory of the day.

            Margaret E. Sangster

The world itself keeps Easter Day,
  And Easter larks are singing;
And Easter flow'rs are blooming gay,
  And Easter buds are springing.
    Alleluia, alleluia.
The Lord of all things lives anew,
  And all His works are living too.
    Alleluia, alleluia.

                John M. Neale

Garden-Fresh Asparagus

Unlike most garden vegetables, asparagus takes two seasons to mature. If you are patient, however, the pleasures received from home-grown garden-fresh asparagus are well worth the wait. These two recipes work best with fresh asparagus; however, if it is not available from the garden (or the market), frozen or canned may be substituted.

Asparagus Pasta Salad
Makes 6 to 8 servings

    1 cup small shell pasta
1½ cups asparagus, cut into 1-inch pieces
½ cup carrots, thinly sliced
½ cup diced onion
¼ cup diced sweet red pepper
½ teaspoon dried oregano
½ cup diced celery
½ to ¾ cup zesty Italian reduced calorie salad dressing

Cook pasta according to package directions. Rinse and drain. Steam asparagus for 4 to 6 minutes. Combine asparagus, carrot, onion, pepper, oregano, and celery. Toss with dressing. Cover and refrigerate for 6 to 8 hours. Serve chilled.

Photos and recipes courtesy The Michigan Asparagus Advisory Board

Asparagus Fiesta Potatoes
Makes 8 servings

  8 large baking potatoes
  1 pound lean ground beef
  1 package taco seasoning mix
3¼ cups asparagus, cut into 1-inch pieces
1½ cups whole kernel corn
  ½ cup diced onion
  ½ cup diced red sweet pepper
  ¼ cup water
  2 cups shredded Monterey-Jack or Cheddar cheese
    Sour cream (optional)

Bake potatoes at 350° for one hour or in microwave oven on high until done. Prepare ground beef with taco seasoning according to package directions. Combine asparagus, corn, onion, sweet pepper, and water; microwave on high for 4 minutes. (Mixture can also be steamed in a small amount of water on top of the stove for 4 to 6 minutes.) Drain vegetables and combine with meat mixture. Continue cooking until asparagus is tender. Cut open baked potatoes and top with asparagus-meat mixture. Sprinkle with cheese and top with sour cream, if desired.

Country CHRONICLE
Lansing Christman

I have always enjoyed nature; but this time of year, as the days grow longer and the evenings stretch out warm and inviting, I'm reminded of another spring many years ago. I often think back to that spring evening and wish that I could return to the same brushy swamp and observe the nocturnal flight of the woodcock, as I did more than sixty-five years ago.

I had seen the woodcock in the swamp during the daylight hours and knew that if I were lucky enough to be there at just the right time, I would be treated to a real show. The swamp was far out in the pasture, beyond the brook. As I walked, the sun slowly set behind the western hills and dusk changed to darkness, but I did not hesitate. I knew the pasture intimately; I knew the swampy lands were filled with hummocks that were always well above the saturated soil of the marsh and I stepped confidently from one to the next.

Finally I arrived at the thicket of woods and took my place on top a huge bolder to wait. I don't know how long I sat there, but at last I saw

what I had been waiting for. The woodcock burst from the trees in his courtship performance and rose high into the sky over the pasture. His wings produced a trill-like song as the bird soared into the air just feet from where I sat.

I had never before witnessed such aerial maneuvers. The bird swooped through the darkening sky, climbing ever higher; and when he could go no further, he paused in the air for a moment and then fell, as though dropped from a hand high above. He leveled out over the trees and glided easily over my head.

The whole performance from beginning to end, left me in awe. It was a delightful experience for a country boy who loved the land, and it made a lasting impression on me. For years, until I grew older and moved far away, I visited the swamp on warm spring evenings as often as possible to enjoy the show.

These long years later, I think about it yet—the thrill, the excitement of that spring twilight moment; the waiting, the watching, the listening—and it is as if I were there. But I am not. I would love to go back there one more time. I would love to once again listen to the song of wings at dusk.

The author of two published books, Lansing Christman has been contributing to Ideals *for almost twenty years. Mr. Christman has also been published in several American, foreign, and braille anthologies. He lives in rural South Carolina.*

Photo Overleaf
GARDEN SPLENDOR
Wilmington Gardens,
Greenfield, North Carolina
Ken Dequaine Photography

A SLICE OF LIFE
— Edgar A. Guest —

Spring Fever

When the blue gets back in the skies once more
And the vines grow green 'round the kitchen door,
When the roses bud and the robins come,
I stretch myself and I say: "Ho hum!
I ought to work but I guess I won't;
Though some want riches to-day, I don't;
This looks to me like the sort of day
That was made to idle and dream away."

When the sun is high and the air just right,
With the trees all blossomy, pink and white,
And the grass, as soft as a feather bed
With the white clouds drifting just overhead,
I stretch and yawn like a school boy then,
And turn away from the walks of men
And tell myself in a shamefaced way:
"I'm going to play hookey from work to-day!"

"Here is a morning too rare to miss,
And what is gold to a day like this,
And what is fame to the things I'll see
Through the lattice-work of a fine old tree?
There is work to do, but the work can wait;
There are goals to reach, there are foes to hate,
There are hurtful things which the smart might say,
But nothing like that shall spoil to-day."

"To-day I'll turn from the noisy town
And just put all of my burdens down;
I'll quit the world and its common sense,
And the things men think are of consequence,
To chum with birds and the friendly trees
And try to fathom their mysteries,
For here is a day which looks to be
The kind I can fritter away on me."

Edgar A. Guest began his illustrious career in 1895 at the age of fourteen when his work first appeared in the Detroit Free Press. *His column was syndicated in over 300 newspapers, and he became known as "The Poet of the People."*

Spring Plays a Harp

Beulah L. Mueller

I opened my door this morning,
And spring was standing there.
Her dress was new; of emerald hue,
And sunshine was her hair.

Her eyes were skies of azure blue,
And she played upon a harp,
A symphony of woodland strains,
Led by a winging lark.

TULIPS
Robert C. Russell, Photographer
International Stock Photos, Inc.

Spring Orchestra

Cleoral Lovell

Bluebells chime and tinkle,
Jonquil trumpets blare,
Honeysuckles sprinkle
Sweet notes into the air.

Tulips rise up, swaying
To a woodwind breeze.
Flowers of spring are playing
Fragrant melodies.

TULIPS
Judy Gurovitz, Photographer
International Stock Photos, Inc.

FROM MY GARDEN JOURNAL

Deana Deck

Picture this scene. On a balmy evening in late spring, dinner's bubbling on the stove and it's time to start the salad. Instead of heading for the refrigerator, you step outside the kitchen door and select fresh greens, a small carrot or two, a radish, and perhaps a scallion or some chives from your salad garden.

Kitchen salad gardens have been around almost as long as there have been homes; and in America as our pioneer ancestors moved west, they carried their favorite "sallet" seeds with them. A kitchen salad garden, even a small one, not only meant fresh vegetables for the family but was a sign of being settled, of being home.

A kitchen salad garden requires very little space and can be grown in a tub or two on the balcony or a sunny patch of ground. With a traditional garden, a raised bed made with railroad ties defines the garden space and allows for more comfortable weeding and harvesting from a sitting position.

Whether your garden is traditional or in balcony tubs, any garden requires plenty of light and rich soil. Dig the soil to a depth of six to eight inches to make a loose seed bed and stir in some 5-10-10 fertilizer, according to package directions. Plant the seeds thickly. The vegetables will be thinned naturally as you pick and eat the early harvest.

Because of different soil temperature requirements for seed germination, not all of the salad produce will be ready at the same time. No matter where you live, however, if you plant varieties suited to the climate, there will be a period of a few weeks in early summer when everything is available at once. For colder climates, a simple cold frame, such as an old storm window over a wide trench or plastic draped over a frame, can greatly extend the life of your garden and allow a second or even third planting of cool season crops. Woven polyester row cover material can be laid directly on the plants and serves the same purpose. It's porous enough to admit sunshine and rain but dense enough to prevent frostbite and insects. This material can also be used to warm the soil and help early plantings germinate quicker.

Because most salad crops grow best in cooler weather, they should be started early. Spinach and lettuce are good cool season crops. In the South, hot weather will kill the crop in early summer, but seeds can be sown again in late summer for a fall crop. The farther north, the longer these greens can be enjoyed; but they will need the protection of a cold frame in spring and fall. And with a cold frame in the South, an early spring crop of spinach and lettuce can be started as early as January!

Snow peas are another cool season crop that can be started in late winter or early spring and enjoyed until hot weather. Snow peas are climbers and can share a simple tripod frame with cucumbers, since the cucumbers mature much later.

Today, with a supermarket on most every corner, a salad garden isn't the necessity it was to our ancestors, but it still says "home" to many of us. With a little advance planning, you can enjoy garden-fresh produce as our ancestors did from the salad garden right outside your kitchen door.

Deana Deck lives in Nashville, Tennessee, where her garden column is a regular feature in the Tennessean.

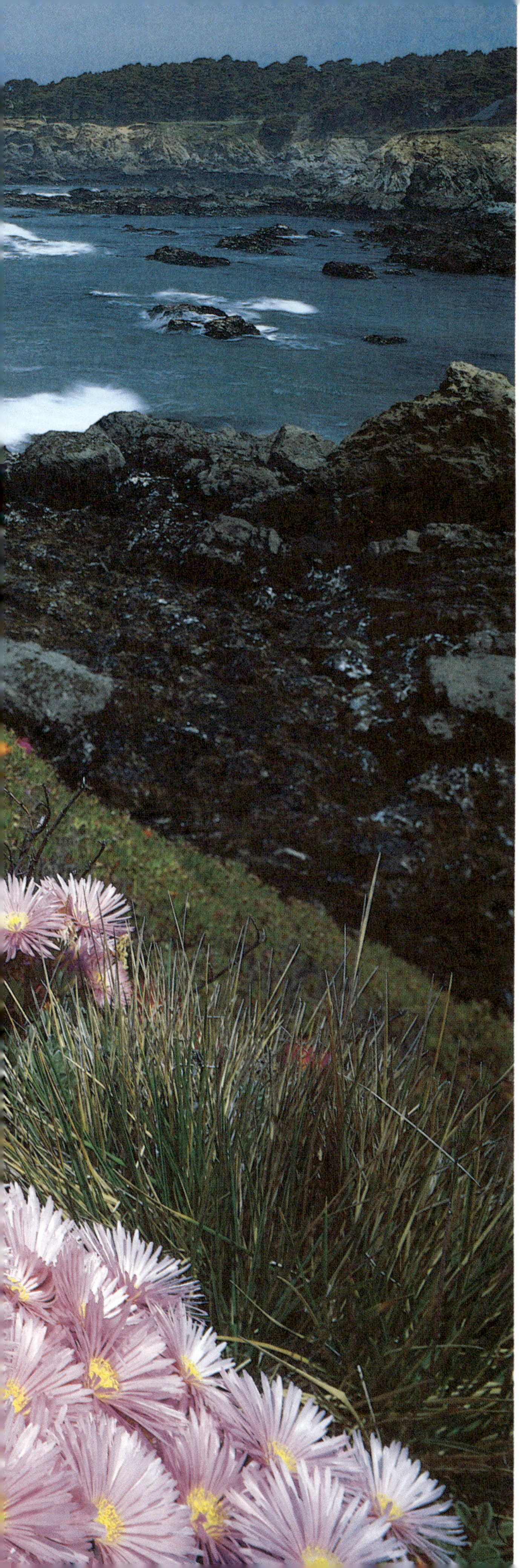

Today

Grace Noll Crowell

I heard God's voice upon the wind today;
I heard Him speaking through the song of birds;
And clearly, plainly, through the silver rain
I heard His words.

I saw God's face upon a flower today;
I saw Him moving on the hills, and oh,
He walked upon the water of the stream,
I know! I know!

I heard God's voice, I saw His shining face;
He spoke to me; He moved along the land;
I reached through all the beauty of the day
And touched His hand.

BOTANICAL GARDENS
Mendocino, California
Ed Cooper, Photographer

THIS EASTER DAY

Loise Pinkerton Fritz

The sun has set behind the hills
This Easter day of daffodils,
Of crocuses and lilies white,
Of tulips with their colors bright.

This Easter day of ringing bells
Resounding over hill and dell,

Proclaiming that there's life anew
When every winter storm is through.

The twilight shades now touch the air
This Easter day of springtime flair,
Of egg hunts in the neighbor's yard,
Of birdsong that uplifts the heart,
Of love that permeates the earth
And pulsates into a rebirth.
The sun, though set with radiant light,
Still glows to light this Easter night.

Readers' Forum

I am honored that you have selected my work for your very fine publication—one of my most favorite and cherished magazines of all time. (I've saved every issue I've ever gotten, from 30+ years ago.)

Linda R. Copper
Baltimore, Maryland

Editor's Note:
You may enjoy Linda's poem "Assurance" in the Reader's Reflection section of this issue.

While growing up at home, my mother had 2 issues of Ideals *magazine—one for Easter and one for Christmas. These were brought out at the appropriate time each year, and when I was little, I loved looking at the beautiful pictures. Growing up brought the joy of being able to read the poems and stories.*

I have always wanted to have that tradition in my home. My mother's magazines had been a gift to her. Three or four years ago, I decided that if I was ever going to have Ideals *in my home, I'd better subscribe myself. So I did.*

I've been able to share them with friends, too. When we are invited to the homes of friends and relatives, I like to take a hostess gift. My first choice for a gift is the current issue of Ideals *if it is available at a . . . bookstore.*

So you see I am not a "new friend," but an old friend who has appreciated and enjoyed Ideals *for a long time.*

Sandy Ehresmann
Plymouth, Minnesota

Editor's Note:
The following is an excerpt from a poem by a subscriber about her pet cat.

My Shuksie

They say senior citizens are ready to be
    laid on the shelf,
But I've got an adorable black cat
    as cute as an elf.

They tell me she is eight years old
    and just sleeps and eats,
But she's full of vim, vigor and vitality
    and she's mine for keeps!

So if you are out of sorts with
    the world and things,
Just get yourself a cat and find out
    what pleasures she brings!

Claire Rhea Hansen
Bellingham, Washington

Claire Rhea Hansen and her pet cat Shuksie

ideals
Celebrating Life's Most Treasured Moments